How to Make a Home Budget
Peter K. Black

Copyright © 2014 Pierre Jereczek

All rights reserved

To my readers and my wonderful wife

Table of Contents

Are your budget always on a diet?

Why budget is everyone's business?

Focus, discipline and commitment.

Commit to easy and practical budgeting.

Step 1: Determine and analyze your source of funds.

Step 2: Defining Your Budget Goals.

Necessities only!

Recreate last month's budget list

Step 3. Do the budget elimination process.

Step 4. Maintain and manage your budget.

Step 5. Spending the budget like there's nothing left.

Step 6. Save the extra and seal it for a month long.

Step 7: Revisiting your budget and change for the better.

Traditional budget methods

Great rewards comes from sheer focus, discipline and determination.

ARE YOUR BUDGET ALWAYS ON A DIET?

Is it something that no matter how you try to make ends meet ends, you're always ending up broke and penniless? And you end up wondering where did you lost track on your budgeting again?

Good news! You are not alone in this kind of feeling. Many home budget are failures on kinds like this. Home budget may seem to sound so tedious and complicated to many but really there is not so much fuzz and flair in budget for the home. But why doing home budgeting make so many a failure and a mess? There could be a hundred and one different reasons as there are fishes in the ocean. But just like any other problem, there is always a solution and a way to solve everything.

Your budget need not always be on a diet if you started on the right track and manage it according to what and how it should be done. But what's so special and unique about home budget that makes it so difficult to many? And to help you understand more the nities of a budget, let's do away with the hard core ones and understand the easy and practical ones. So let's start with the basics!

Why budget is everyone's business?

Why not? As you take deep in focusing about your household budget, you might want to know why budget is essential to every home and everyone:

- ✓ Improve one's health. Managing an efficient budget can release you from stress and worries on how your budget is spent.
- ✓ Managing budget can improve one's judgement and disposition. Efficient budgeting will improve your disposition in handling money matters. You will be able to come up with ideas on how to effectively stretch your money to the limits without overspending or breaking your goals and funds.
- ✓ You will have better spending habits. It is quite interesting and noteworthy to know your spending habits in the end will be your gauge in changing for the better and attain effective financial management not only in your homes but in almost everything you're going to deal involving money matters.
- ✓ You will be able to manage your debts and loans efficiently.
- ✓ You will be able to develop an emergency fund and plan as cushion if you fail.

- ✓ You will be able to device a workout plan for repayments of your debts and loans.

- ✓ Improves financial creativity. You will be amazed on how you will learn to be creative in dealing with ways to augment and sustain the limited fund of a home budget. You will be able to refrain from luxury living into a more simple and practical one.

- ✓ Improve sustainability. Ultimately, doing your budget can lead you to attain financial sustainability through wise investment and other money making machines.

- ✓ You will become money masters. When you take budget skilfully, you not only manage your budget efficiently but you'll become money experts as well.

- ✓ Failures won't hurt you because you will be able to develop your 'Never give up!' motivation.

The possibilities of improvement in all areas of running a household budget are limitless. And you just need three basic skills to start management of a diet home budget.

Focus, discipline and commitment.

You need focus because this is your household budget and everything in it are vital to your family's daily sustenance and needs. It is therefore important that your undivided focus in managing the household budget is working perfectly. Your moves should always be in line with your prime directives so your budget won't fail. A home budget should always focus on what's good and best for your family.

Just like any other types of setting up goals, home budget is as important as any budget there is. It does not need to be complex like that of a corporate planned budget, but home budget is the core in every home finances and an integral part of every homemaker's world. Ideally we do a home budget to satisfy and achieve the household goals we wanted to have with less effort but effective options to free us away from the hassles and worries of a busy household. Where the main focus is manage the household yet keep an efficient yet balanced home finances utilizing only the limited money resources coming in.

An efficiently managed home budget can liberate you from the headaches and burdens brought about by a mismanaged home finances. But before you can totally be burden free from managing your home finances, you must learn how to effectively handle planning, setting up goals and efficiently spend or allot every penny you have. But how would you do budgeting when you are facing a blank wall and don't know where to start?

In this budget series, we will show you how a sound yet easy and practical way how to do a budget that could set free you from the hassles and troubles of getting broke and penniless. Whether you're a busy homemaker, a student or a home alone mongrel, this series will definitely nail you to stick to your budget and be financially wise and independent. We will try to inspire, equip and challenge you on how you can make your budget look the way that you believe it should be, without necessarily deviating from what you have initially planned or set to accomplish in your budget. The series deals not only to small time budgeting but can also be applied to big ones with just a little tweak on the goals, the items for budget and the manner of execution.

COMMIT TO EASY AND PRACTICAL BUDGETING.

Simple budgeting for beginners need not be that complicated and long. It is better and easier to practice budgeting in easy practical terms. What is important is your focus, determination and commitment to achieve your goal of managing the household budget to its fullest and practical way so you can concentrate more on earning for keeps rather than spending it foolishly. If you're a beginner and new in doing home budget, you full commitment is a wise move since anything that is new and requires monitoring must be done with the right motivation and dedication.

Let's go!

STEP 1: DETERMINE AND ANALYZE YOUR SOURCE OF FUNDS.

In many budget starters, the first thing that comes in their mind are the items they wanted to buy with the ready money they have. But, let's do away with the traditional and let's look first into your funds and sources. What are some pointers why you need to analyse your source of budget fund?

- ❖ Your budget fund must always be the money you have physically on hand. Thinking you only have actual limited cash will drive that motivation to limit your purchase.

- ❖ It is easy to set a budget fund that is readily available. So use a fund that is set ahead of time. Don't rely on your current or incoming funds. This way, your current income and future incoming funds will be your backup funds and cushion if you fall really short for this period's budgeting. Use your fund sources one period at a time. If you constantly practice this, you will have an easy budget management for your home.

- ❖ Refrain from getting and thinking of using your credit card limit as your budget fund. This will just create a clout in your mind that although you have a credit limit, you have the option to extend your purchase to a credit which if you fail to monitor could get you into more debts to the card company.

- ❖ It is advisable to use your DEBIT card instead of your CREDIT card. Your debit card automatically deducts and update the actual value you spent unto your bank while shopping thereby doing away with service charges from the card company. If it has, it'll only be a minimum service amount called interchange, discount or maintenance fee charged by your bank.

- ❖ If your budget fund is from salaries, you need to put into your mind that your fund replenishes only on periodic basis that is every month or whenever the term of your salaries maybe. This will help you control your shopping limit since, the next opportunity could only come on the next payroll term. You may need to assess if the item you're buying will last within the term of the current pay period.

STEP 2: DEFINING YOUR BUDGET GOALS.

In a home budget, it is very important to define what do we really need and what are those we just wanted to have. There is a BIG difference in doing budget for what you need than plan a budget for what you just simply want. In setting up your budget goals

A **NEED** is something you are to accomplish with priority and urgency, whereas a **WANT** is a goal you can accomplish with less urgency and could still be alternatively modify or defer to settle in another time or way. In budgeting it is however advisable to want what you need NOT need what you want.

Ideally, a food budget is for a week or a month's food consumption. By focusing on what your needs are rather than what you want, you will now be able to list down the items you are going to assign the money for the budget. Other than food budget, other goals are simply on a need, secondary and non-essentials. As you go through managing your budget, these non-essentials will play a lot and will even act as your fall back to augment and help you get through your periodic budget activity. As you master planning and setting on rules on your budget there are a number of items and ways that you wouldn't believe will be the answer to manipulate and manage your budget. Your creative skills coupled with planning and sound judgement are personal skills you will be using a lot within the budget term.

NECESSITIES ONLY!

Your budget should always first focus on what's necessary and prime. With the limited money you have on hand, list down all that's necessary and important such as food, medicines, bills, school fees, insurances and other priorities. These listed needs are your budget goals essential and necessary.

A typical example of a budget goal or necessity is your food budget. It can further be broken down into several sub categories such as: home meals, food allowances for work and school as well as dining out food budget.

TIP: Don't list down what you can't accommodate on your limited budget. During the elimination process in Step 4, it could be very frustrating to see that they will be eliminated and cannot be accommodated. So avoid frustrations by doing critical judgement.

Try to do it one step at a time. It's always healthy to practice and analyse using your gut and critical thinking. Because if you will later face a similar situation, you can render sound judgement wisely.

Recreate last month's budget list

A practical way to cut down your time and effort on listing down your budget is recreating last month's list and try to improve it. Eliminate from the list what you still have enough to last this month's consumption and add on to those that needed upgrades. As a rule of thumb, what you have listed and spent last month is most likely what you will list and spend this month.

Even with a tight money to budget with always remember the following:

- ✓ Quality over quantity. It is best that you buy the healthiest, the freshest and food items really needed by your family.
- ✓ Do always bring the grocery list while shopping and limit buying only what's on the list.
- ✓ Always check on labels and ingredients for health and ingredients only fitted for your family
- ✓ Never buy expired or nearly expired food products and always check security of food containers.
- ✓ Eat a full meal in the house before shopping. An empty stomach would lead you only to consider eating out which could ruin your tight budgeting. You need discipline to curtail your personal urges and whims.

Remember, you don't want to buy food items that will be a threat to your family's health. A value commitment to your family that you will only serve them healthy food even on a tight budget. You need commitment to spend your hard earned money wisely. And now that you have everything you need to get going. Let's do it.

Ready, Set Goals!

STEP 3. DO THE BUDGET ELIMINATION PROCESS.

Although typically very tricky but not necessary if you are accustomed with your regular budget goals, budget elimination will further streamline your budget goals according to urgency of needs since some items by reason and significance can still be deferred or delayed in some other time or period depending on the immediate urgency. But bear in mind that a budget value has to be assigned and earmarked and need to be still accomplished as they are still listed as necessary and needed by your family. A typical example of this budget need is small house fixes. It's either you fix it yourself or wait for the next budget funding so long as it does not pose any immediate threat to your family like leaking faucet, fence repair, new set of uniforms, etc. They are necessary yet a little time of deferral in favour of available budget fund can still be negligible. Flexibility on some items can be allowed but always bear in mind to stick to your goal and never deviate from it. A few unexpected yet necessary items might be inserted along the way but setting a rule will prevent you from overshooting off your budget. Set a certain percentage for these unexpected items but the earmarked value must not exceed the proportional value against the total allotted value of your particular budget goal where it belongs. Anything beyond it will pose a threat of not realizing or achieving desired result of your budget goal. So be very careful. Again, focus, discipline and determination drives you through your budget, so stay in tune with your goals.

STEP 4. MAINTAIN AND MANAGE YOUR BUDGET.

Keep a record of your budget to aid you in analysing what needs improvement later on. Revisit and adjust. At this point, budget failures are not impossible but take on

Assign a value to each of the item on your goal list. It could be a value you already have knowledge that is worth for the item, or a best assumption based on popular search or practical living info. Never be afraid to exercise your best gut, who knows it could be the best possible option. So, give it your best shot.

TIP3: You can get practical value of every budget item in the net, newspaper, magazines and other media. As time goes by, your skill in assigning value to your budget items will improve and be good in it as you practice budgeting on your own.

STEP 5. SPENDING THE BUDGET LIKE THERE'S NOTHING LEFT.

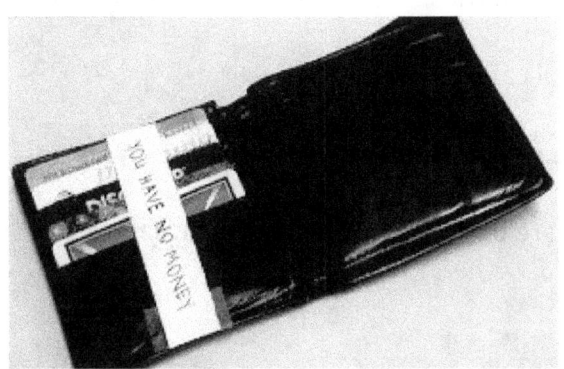

Make it a motivation that before leaving the house to buy the needed items. Assume practicing in your mind that what you have in your wallet is the most of it and no extra for overspending. This way you keep your focus on the budget and be as frugal as possible while spending it. Even if what you are to buy offers a trip to the moon if you buy it. Choose living on Earth for the next century with what you can only buy with your budget money no matter what. Avoid being in a situation of losing ends. Take serious notes on the following:

- Do not practice compulsive buying. This will only get you into more debts and money problems. Think and analyse before you commit to buying.
- Do not make shopping your cure for stress. Bonding with the kids or your pets has more healthy benefits than shopping in terms of stress and anxiety treatment.
- Pay your bills in full and on time. A good creditor is always a great customer where rewards are given just by accomplishing your duty to pay your bills on time. Credit card companies at times give extra incentives to their prompt paying customers.

- Pay in cash and not your credit cards. This is the primary role of why you do budgeting. So you can do away with all your debt-creating worries. Who need credit cards if you can efficiently run your budget and pay in cool cash!
- Make practical habits like riding the bus instead of your own car, cook your own meals, be your own handy man in the house. These are basics that are sure practical measures to save your hard earned money.

Spending your budget money wisely can take in almost every way possible. Some of the great ideas from home makers and shopping addicts are really practical and easy to follow if you really want to stay in line with your budget:

- Coupons and discounts. Make coupon and discount clipping your hobby and past time. Grab and use coupons and discounts for your purchases. A variety of media fortnightly publish some as a click marketing campaign and all you have to do is grab the opportunity. Never be afraid to try any of them for who knows it might be the only solution you need to augment your very thin budget.
- Best time to go shopping. Periodically, commercial shopping entities always campaign for event sales on their establishment to attract crowd and sales. Typical examples are holiday sales, inventory sales, closing out sales, etc. All you have to do is monitor when will be the next event and seize it.
- Garage sales. Bazaars, community neighbourhood rummage sales are simply another way to help you save. If are not solve with the idea on buying or, visiting one could spark an idea for your business minded mind. Who knows you might bump in with your

next business partner so it is not really that bad, right? Calendar every garage sales, bazaars and other sales event. And make every venue of your social and business meetings within.

- ✓ Organize your stuff. Organization will also help your mind clutter-free and have a better perspective in managing your home budget. And as part of home organization, mastering stock piling wisely will not only make your homes look great but will aid you in easily finding things in the house. Practice being a minimalist not only on your budget but in also in speeding up the ways to get you through your budget easily. The lesser steps and procedures

- ✓ Group dining and chipping. Participating with friends and family with group dining and chipping helps you to stretch the spending capabilities of your budget money.

- ✓ Budget like a big rich spender but spend like a frugal wise man. Budget on what you like best but spending the minimal to get it is a sweet reward for your home budgeting. Tasting and experiencing what you have bought at amazingly low price is like the feeling of winning in a lottery. Sometimes you just couldn't imagine yourself how you did it. But you did it anyway! Isn't that amazing?

- ✓ Liberate yourself and attain financial freedom from budget worries. And the most beneficial is your freedom from all the worries about your financial problems.

STEP 6. SAVE THE EXTRA AND SEAL IT FOR A MONTH LONG.

This is a must and should always be after Step 3. Why the minimum of a full month savings? This is because the money you save can only earn interest after a full month. This serves as your cushion for any adjustment. And how much it earned is how much adjustment you can have. Thus, if you have any other options to have that budget extra grow and earn, seize it! It could add up to your opportunity to give a better budget allotted for such item. Otherwise, stay focus on the month long saving and move on.

Below are some practical ways to invest your extra budget money:

- ✓ Deposit to the bank to earn interest. Short term CDs may not be that big interest earners but the idea is to get your fund into safety and still have that confidence in thinking you still have money in case you fall short of everything. It's basically a safety net at the back of your mind.

- ✓ Invest in short-term money market funds like time deposit, stock options, treasury bills and other short term money plans.

Investing your money into some of the available money making instruments are wise moves to earn, add up, replenish and serve as your reserve funds. Just be very cautious in the details of each instrument and know every catch or loop holes by asking experts, research and observing money trends. Some people try to play low profile in taking the risks but as a rule of thumb for still inexperienced and new learners, being conservative and practical can get you through in avoiding risks. For in reality everything has a certain price of risks, one just need to practice sound judgement to bring you into the myriads of the money market arena. But once you breeze out everything and smoothen your dealings, your budget is just something so common to do and easy routine. The important thing is that you take charge and master your skills, move and continue to the next level of management and mastering your home finances. Just keep focus and maintain on money making instruments that will give you a steady stream of passive inflows to sustain your funds. One of the common fails of a home budget is the lack of sustainable passive funds and only focus on a single source like the monthly or weekly pay. This has to be changed for the better. There are other options offered by other Institutions like banks, cooperatives, and trusts. Even the internet is thriving with unlimited options and sources of funds. You just need to tap your every potential to work out these possibilities.

Step 7: Revisiting your budget and change for the better.

Remember that practice makes perfect. A budget need not be that complicated to do but the practice offers unlimited rewards to anybody who takes it in focus and seriously thinking about every financial goal they wanted to achieve. It is a must routine for everyone that can lead to high yields not only to you, your family but to the economy as a whole. What is important is your effort and initiative to work out your personal and home finances and release you from the burdens most home makers have suffered with managing their home budget. At this point you must be able to do the following that will aid you in easily going through a limited diet home budget:

- ✓ Identify loose ends and areas of improvement;
- ✓ Increase your savings and investment skills;
- ✓ You will be more realistic and optimistic;
- ✓ Easily manage loans and debts;
- ✓ Easily adjust and fine tune your budget.
- ✓ You will learn how to evaluate
- ✓ You will be able to render sound estimates and projections;
- ✓ You will be able to plan ahead and decide accordingly;
- ✓ You will develop and improve your problem solving abilities;
- ✓ You will develop a more positive outlook in terms of financial constraints and issues;
- ✓ You will be able to live within your means.
- ✓ You will be able to track and evaluate your current spending and stay within the rules you set within.
- ✓ You will be able to discover other means to save and spend your money wisely;
- ✓ You will develop strong discipline and get used in avoiding shopping and spending temptations;
- ✓ You will be less worry free and confident on the outcome of your budget.
- ✓ You will have more time to spend with your family and other activities.
- ✓ You will not be afraid to fail since you have made measures to cushion your budget should it fail.

Keep track of your goals and get up to date updates by revisiting and improving your techniques. Your practical life experiences are a good source of your ways on how to improve it. Advices and keeping up to date with info from the media and other homemakers are good sources too and will help you improve and tailor your ability.

Traditional Budget Methods

Remember that you don't need a budget that's always on a diet if you have the right nutritional elements to nourish it. Do not be afraid to fail for doing the budget is a recurring pattern. Sometimes the outcome aren't those the ones we plan and hoped due to some valid factors. Trying out again and again is a learning process necessary to change the plan for the better. And one way to improve your home budget management is try to manage it on a different approach. Below are some popular yet practical ways to manage your home budget. These methods are somewhat traditional but they are effective simple approach that can easily be followed by any person who want to do some low impact budgeting. These traditional and simple budget systems can likewise be applied to home budgeting but on a more personal approach. The use of some traditional tools will aid in managing the entire budget system in a somewhat old fashioned way. Remember no budget method is that perfectly tailored to suit everyone's way but managing a home budget need some form of your own creative touch to personalize it. Others may not agree but just laugh it out for it is something you alone can do and make. A unique trade secret you can forever keep and treasure as you share the bounty and reaps with your loved ones.

The 6 Money Jar System

The 6 money jar system of saving is the equivalent of the Harv Eker's How to Get Rich Series on saving through frugality. Each money jar was assigned a budget goal and was given a share or percentage of the budget. Each was labelled accordingly as follows. In labelling you can instead assign your own personalized label to replace each:

NEC Jar - NEC stands for necessity items.

FFA Jar   - FFA stands for Financial Freedom Account.

EDU Jar - EDU stands for Educational funds

LTSS Jar - LTSS stands for Long Term Savings for Spending

PLAY Jar – PLAY stands for itself

CHARITY Jar - CHARITY says it all

The basic idea is to earmark a certain sum or percentage of your budget fund and locked it in the jar as the only money you are to spend in each goal label accordingly.

Budgeting With Envelopes

A variation of the 6 Money Jar system, instead of using bulky and fragile jars, envelopes are used to store and assign value to each of the budget goals.

These traditional budget yet effective goal assigning has been varied in so many ways and in different terms all across the globe, Others uses, piggy banks, pocket holes, cookie jars, bamboo poles, cash boxes and even opening each of the goals a bank account, debit or credit card. Sometimes it just takes your own creativity to motivate you so you can manage your budget. In home budget the ways of securing your financial sustainability to gain total control of your budget money always has to stay with the basic motivation of focus, discipline and commitment without breaking and ruining your budget goals. And to aid you further and hone your skills for the better, revisiting and making your ways to change and improve management of your budget take merits for you to be a skilled money master and survivor in the world of wise spenders!

Budgeting with a pen and a paper (or Excel)

How to build a Day to Day Budget?

1) Step 1: Track all your expenses

    We've seen that you have to make a list of all your expenses during a year.

    You have to estimate all your costs: your housing costs, food, utilities, clothing, medical expenses, family expenses, transportation and vehicle costs, entertainment and activities, payment debts priorities, other expenses and saving for in case of emergency.

    Since it's down, you have to structure it:

2) Step 2: Structure your budget

    Ok, now you have a huge list. Putting it down under categories will improve it a lot.

    Make two columns, one with the categories you've listed, and put in front of them the total amount.

    You'll have something like this:

Expenses	Total
Housing	
Food	
Utilities	
Clothing	

Medical	
Family	
Transports	
Activities	
Holidays	
Debts	
Saving	
Total	

3) Step 3: Don't forget to monitor and review your budget

Your budget should be flexible, and to be flexible you have to make reviews from time to time. If you don't review it, you'll lose with it.

4) Step 4: Keep being well informed

There are tons of budgeting tips, tools and information on the Internet, you have to know what is a credit, how it works, what is a medical insurance, did you find the right one for your needs? And so on.

5) Step 5: Make budgeting a happy activity

To make your budget doesn't have a painful activity and the sign of a lot of restrictions. The budgeting process will make new habits and you'll know where your money is going.

It can be a game, to optimize your expenses, to try to increase your saving, etc.

GREAT REWARDS COMES FROM SHEER FOCUS, DISCIPLINE AND DETERMINATION.

In home budgeting, no matter what type of methods you do primitive or not, your focus to uphold and maintain everything you've planned on your budget goals is the prime directive and making each a success. In today's world of so many temptations, many people run out of options and submerge themselves in debts soaring high even up to their eyeballs and sometimes beyond their heads. Why do you need to join them if you have all the means and skills to liberate yourself from getting into it?

The key to the money jar and envelope system is that when the jar or envelope goes empty, you are done spending for that period and forces you to plan and think ahead based on how much money you can only go. Discipline is something that will effectively work along with these systems. Frugality does not mean you have to strangle yourself with extreme spending habits. Spending wise and practical is a way and means to a better living condition and pampering you and your household with what is best in the most economical and practical way.

Whether you use the traditional or the sophisticated way to do your home budget, your basic motivation should always go hand on hand with every step of the way. Focus on your goals, discipline on doing your ways and commitment to manage and make your every budget goal a success! Congratulations and applaud yourself.

Having a limited budget does not mean you have to keep everything in tight measures all the time. But once you laid all the foundations of your budget and you've come to master the three fundamental skills of focus, discipline and determination, a smooth and easy sailing leading to a rewarding achievement of your goals not only become a sweet journey experience but more on having a relaxed budgeting with a steady flow of funding options that will definitely make you a true survivor wise spender from the bondage of financial restraints. You may not have every material luxury items every royalty has but you can definitely live in harmony and with peace of mind that even royalties are trying so hard to achieve. Something no money can buy. Something nobody can take away from you.

Managing a home budget will not only make you masters in the four corners of your home but will even get you a step ahead in any battle of finances and emerge victorious holding the shield of paper and pen in a calculator armour with a wise laurel on your head. Rejoice for you are one true rare treasure and breed. A real super hero in the financial world!

www.ingramcontent.com/pod-product-compliance
Lightning Source LLC
Chambersburg PA
CBHW081805170526
45167CB00008B/3331